I Left You a PRESENT

ROBB PEARLMAN

CIDER MILL PRESS

BOOK PUBLISHERS

KENNEBUNKPORT, MAINE

Introduction

Dogs provide us with a never-ending supply of presents. Whether it's excited and wet licks on our faces when we come home, never-long-enough cuddles in our beds when we struggle to wake up, or a misplaced poop when and where we least expect it, our trusted companions can be counted on to fill our lives with friendship, surprises, laughs, and, most importantly, unconditional adoration. And when we take the time to look, we'll notice a certain twinkle in their eyes—undeniable proof that there's even more to them than we, as mere humans, could ever imagine. The dogs in this collection all have something to say. But, like your own treasured pup, what they really mean is "I love you."

Here. Next time can you *not* throw it in the lake?

I... I don't think I like your tone.

Teeheehee! They'll never guess where I buried the car keys!

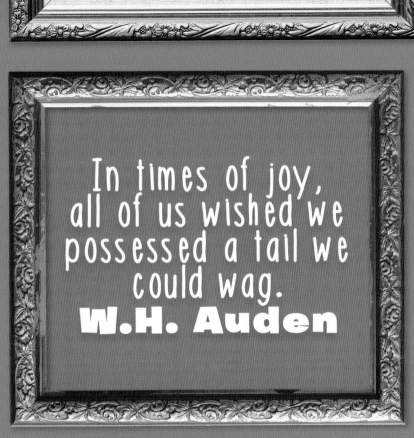

In times of joy,
all of us wished we
possessed a tail we
could wag.

W.H. Auden

If you need me,
I'll be in my room.

So refreshing!

The most affectionate creature in the world is a wet dog.

Ambrose Bierce

Flower gardens. Come for the pee, stay for the comfort.

What? It's called "fertilizer"!

I don't care! What do *you* want to do today?

Yes. This. *This* is the place.

I have to make it *and* clean it up?

I'm too pooped to party.

Almost... almost...

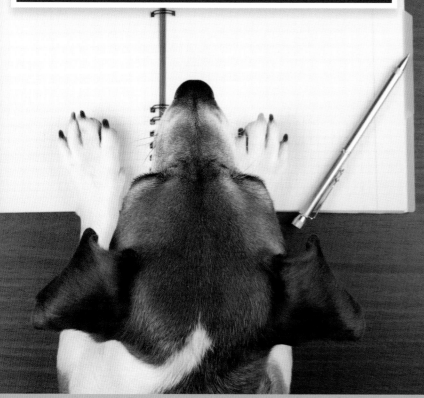

I don't mind taking the blame, but shouldn't you actually do *some* homework?

Doggone *right* I catch like a girl!

I hope you kept the receipt.

Just... a... little... bit... more...

The better I get to know men, the more I find myself loving dogs.

Charles de Gaulle

I made the bed!

A little privacy, please?

It's Sunday. I don't care about the Henderson account, and neither should you.

I'm so embarrassed.

Listen, Elf. You can't stay on that shelf forever.

Guys! GUYS! You gotta try this. You go in one end, and you wind up in a totally different place!

I left you a present!

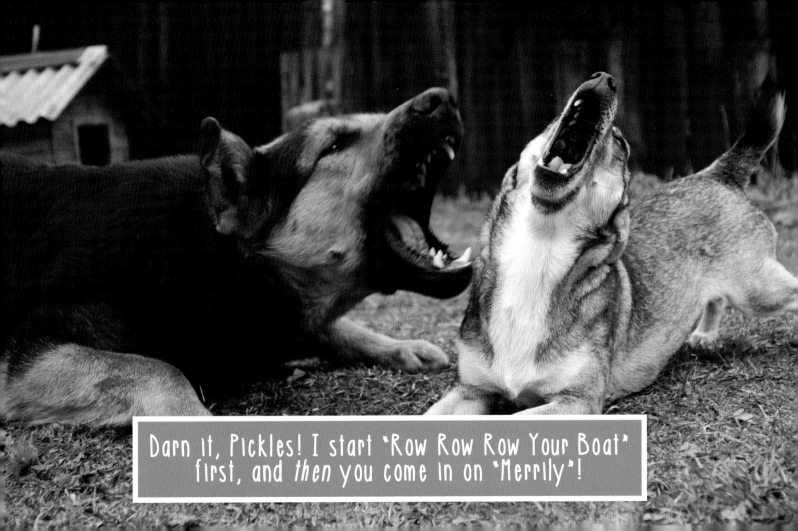

I see you out there, cat. I see you.

Did I hear a can opening?

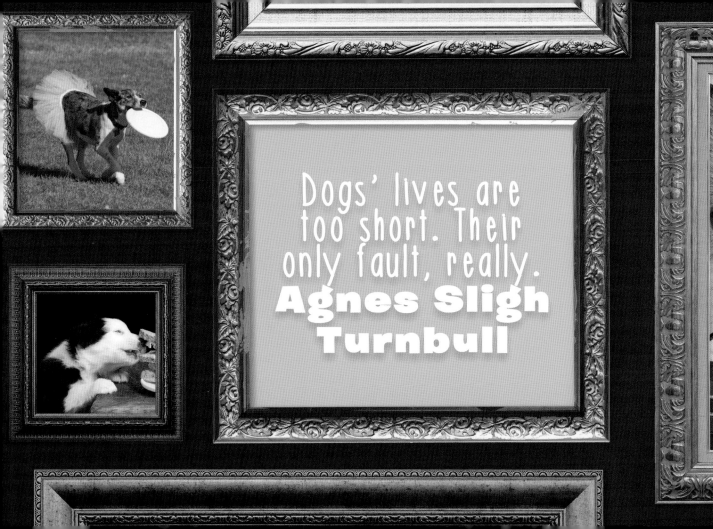

Dogs' lives are too short. Their only fault, really.
Agnes Sligh Turnbull

I don't know what all this white stuff is, but I love it.

Can I come with you?

Leave the penthouse? Please.

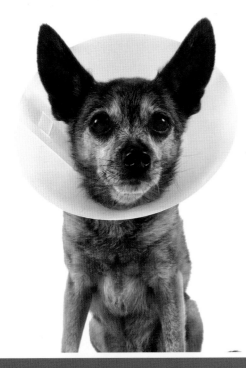

The last thing I remember is you telling me that we were going out for a cone.

I believe it was Coco Chanel who said "One should always remove one accessory before leaving the house."

Would you *please* just ask for directions?

Mom? Mom! MOM! We have to go potty.

I'm here for the belly rubs.

Dogs and philosophers do the greatest good and get the fewest rewards.

Diogenes

There's no such thing as too matchy-matchy.

Kids these days...

NOW I'm the cutest.

All clear, but you forgot to pack underwear.

But I wanna go over theeeeerrrreeeee!

Say hello to my little friend.

I'm helping do the laundry!

Mondays, ammiright?

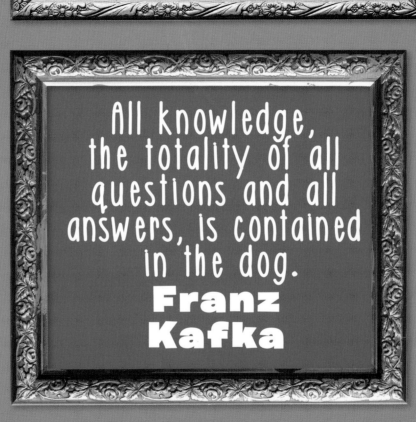

All knowledge,
the totality of all
questions and all
answers, is contained
in the dog.
Franz Kafka

Martha! How lovely to see you, darling. Is this new? I love it.

Atta girl.

He did it.

Playing. Eating. Sleeping. It's exhausting!

Wait, lemme think. A treat? Are you thinking of a treat? I'm thinking of a treat.

Obedience School yearbook photos are all the rage.

I was trying to recycle.

So. You're the new guy.

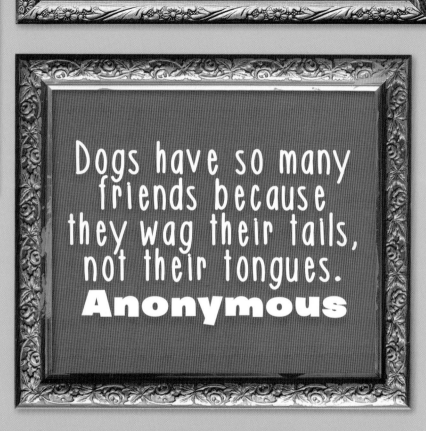

Dogs have so many friends because they wag their tails, not their tongues.
Anonymous

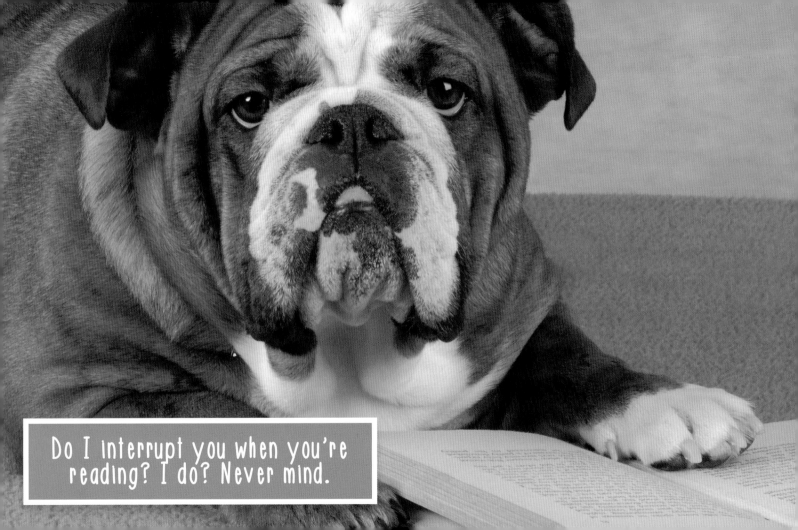

Do I interrupt you when you're reading? I do? Never mind.

Let me show you how to shake hands.

Let me help you with the dishes.

You've got a lot to learn, kid.

Don't tell anyone, but the cuter we are, the more treats we'll get.

You're coming back, right?

Let me get this straight. I make it *outside*, and then you pick it up and bring it *inside*?

A barking dog is often more useful than a sleeping lion.

Washington Irving

You dropped your Frisbee again.
Lemme get that for you.

It's you and me, kid. You and me.

I'm a cowdog! I'm a cowdog!

Let every toy fear...the Masked Chewer!

Whoever loveth me, loveth my hound.

Sir Thomas More

This will look
divine in the den.

Well, ball. You've won this round.

Where are we going?
Where are we going?
Where are we going?

I'm so glad she splurged for the quilted kind.

Uh-oh. He found my present. At least he'll never find me here.

ABOUT THE AUTHOR

Robb Pearlman is the proud owner of Oscar, the most adorable puppy in the history of adorable puppies. He's also the author of *The Wit and Wisdom of Star Trek*, *Fun with Kirk and Spock*, *Movie Night Trivia*, and other pop culture titles.

ABOUT CIDER MILL PRESS BOOK PUBLISHERS

Good ideas ripen with time. From seed to harvest, Cider Mill Press brings fine reading, information, and entertainment together between the covers of its creatively crafted books. Our Cider Mill bears fruit twice a year, publishing a new crop of titles each spring and fall.

CIDER MILL
PRESS

BOOK
PUBLISHERS

VISIT US ON THE WEB AT
www.cidermillpress.com

OR WRITE TO US AT
12 Spring Street
PO Box 454
Kennebunkport, Maine 04046